Discovering OLD BUSES AND TROLLEYBUSES

David Kaye

Shire Publications Ltd.

CONTENTS

 First published May, 1972. ISBN 0 85263154 5.

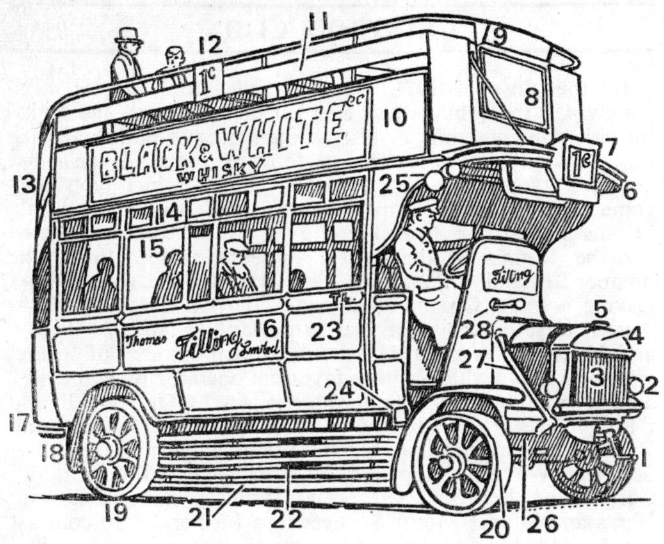

DIAGRAM OF A 1923 DOUBLE-DECKER
(Front Off-Side view)

Description of numbered parts

Part No.	Description
1.	Starting handle
2.	Head lamp
3.	Radiator grille
4.	Chassis manufacturer's name plate (sometimes operator's name substituted)
5.	Radiator filler cap
6.	Driver's canopy
7.	Route number plate in slot
8.	Via destination board in slot
9.	Final destination board in slot
10.	Advert panel (formerly 'decency board')
11.	Guard rails
12.	Route number plate in slot
13.	Staircase
14.	Lower saloon ventilation windows
15.	Lower saloon windows (non-opening)
16.	Fleet legend on lower panels
17.	Platform
18.	Mudguard
19.	Wooden spoked wheel
20.	Solid rubber tyre
21.	Five-bar life guard
22.	Petrol tank (under chassis)
23.	Running number on stencil
24.	Driver's foot step
25.	Driving mirror
26.	Front dumb iron (chassis end)
27.	Steering column
28.	Horn

1. INTRODUCTION

By the close of 1971 over 80 trolleybuses and approximately 450 motorbuses had escaped the scrapyard and ended up either in museums or else in the hands of enthusiasts. In this book we hope to have a look at some of the more common types of buses and trolleybuses, which you may come across at rallies. For instance, whereas the one and only Dennis 'Pelican' single-decker of 1956 has just been purchased for the Dennis Brothers' new museum at Guildford, the unique Leyland 'Panda' of 1940 has disappeared without leaving a trace. On the other hand 50 AEC 'Regents' are at present in safe keeping, as are 56 Leyland 'Titans', 28 'Tigers' and 22 'Lions'. A great deal depends upon the area of Britain you live in as to whether your favourite operator is represented amongst the ranks of these vehicles. 56 LGOC, LPTB and LTE vehicles are in custody, and from elsewhere in the South Devon General accounts for 17 preserved vehicles, as does Southern/Western National, whilst further east Bournemouth Corporation has attracted preservationists in 14 cases and Hants and Dorset Motor Services in a further 12. In contrast few United Automobile Services buses have been saved, and only one (to the author's knowledge) from Northern General Transport's fleet.

If the reader wants to find out more about the vehicles he finds at rallies or in museums, then he should buy or borrow some of the volumes listed in the bibliography. The amount written on old buses and trolleybuses increases yearly, and a subscription to a magazine like *Buses* is well worth while, if you want to keep pace with the preservation scene.

Not all the vehicles listed in this book have yet been restored to a condition in which they would be roadworthy enough to appear at rallies. Neither does every society licence all their vehicles each year, since at £25 p.a. per vehicle this would be too expensive a process.

Readers are asked, please, to admire vehicles from the outside, unless asked on board. Please remember, too, that any souvenirs that you might be tempted to take away with you mean that that vehicle can no longer be enjoyed in its entirety by other enthusiasts. When you realise that it may take as long as four years to restore a vehicle, you can imagine how heartbreaking the loss of parts is to those who have sacrificed so much of their leisure time.

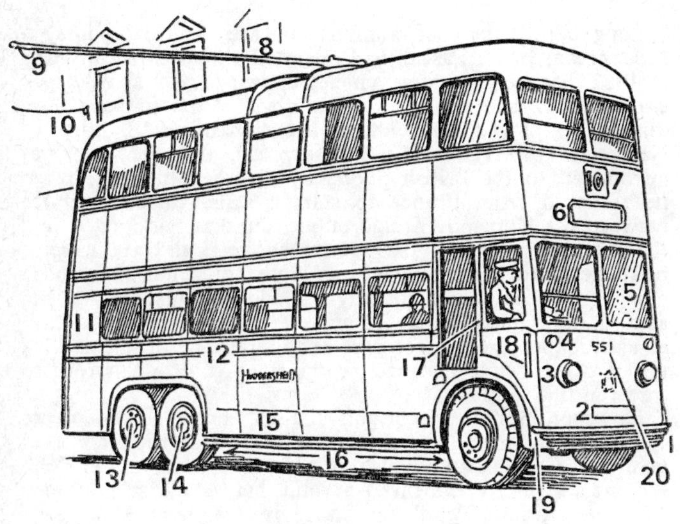

DIAGRAM OF A 1948 SIX-WHEELER TROLLEYBUS
(Front Off-Side view)

Description of numbered parts

Part No.	Description
1.	Chrome strip front bumper
2.	Registration number plate
3.	Head lamp
4.	Side light
5.	Front bulk-head (in this case enclosed within the 'fully-fronted' bodywork)
6.	Destination blind
7.	Route number blind
8.	Trolley booms
9.	Trolley heads on overhead

Part No.	Description
10.	Span wire attached to wall bracket
11.	Enclosed rear staircase with luggage compartment beneath
12.	Waist band
13.	Live axle (i.e. driving axle)
14.	Trailing axle
15.	Battery compartments
16.	Wheelbase
17.	Sliding cab door
18.	Trafficator
19.	Front wing
20.	Fleet number

2. THE DEVELOPMENT OF THE OMNIBUS

Long before the first omnibus appeared in this country a Frenchman, Blaise Pascal, had operated a bus service in Paris in 1662 using eight-seater vehicles known locally as *carrosses à cinq sous*. The actual title 'omnibus' seems to have been initially employed by another Frenchman, M. Baudry of Nantes in 1819. Hence it is not surprising that the word was introduced to the British public by George Shillibeer, when he returned from France to start a stage carriage service between the Yorkshire Stingo public house at Paddington and the Bank on 4th July 1829. Since bookings did not have to be made in advance, and since anybody could join the vehicle along the route, it was literally a mode of transport 'for all', as its Latin name suggests. Mind you, it was necessary to have at least sixpence (2½p) for part of the journey, or one shilling (5p) for the whole distance, so the poor could not afford to travel in this fashion.

However, Shillibeer's original 22-seat single-deckers (plate 1), pulled by three horses abreast, were not the first local vehicles to run in an English city, for five years earlier John Greenwood had commenced a route between Market Street, Manchester, and Pendleton, using twelve-seater short-stage coaches. Strangely enough, whereas Shillibeer changed to smaller two-horse vehicles, Greenwood substituted his first buses with three-horse high-capacity buses. The 1832 Stage Carriage Act legalised the picking up of passengers anywhere in the street, and soon the number of vehicles running in London mushroomed. Roof seats seemed to have appeared c. 1845, and with the stimulus of the 1851 Great Exhibition many more double-deckers took to the streets of the metropolis. At the same time fares were drastically cut, so that penny stages were introduced.

These first double-deckers were known as 'knifeboards', since their long back-to-back seat on the top deck was like a Victorian knifeboard. The standard number of seats for the second half of the nineteenth century was 26. Then in 1881 the London Road Car Company introduced the first 'garden seat' double-decker, in which the seats were arranged in pairs facing forward on the top deck. During this whole period, however, the normal seating plan for the lower deck was for long bench-type seats running along the sides.

In his book *The Story of Passenger Transport in Britain* James Joyce gives an excellent description of the typical garden-seat bus:

'There was of course no heating. The best they could do in this direction was a mass of straw on the floor, and this was intended not only as some kind of insulation to keep your feet warm, but also as a general repository for mud and any other variety of dirt that might find its way downwards.'

Since ladies had begun to sit on the top deck, so-called 'decency boards' were fitted to the otherwise open sides, so that peeping Toms might not obtain an illicit glance at a revealed ankle. The conductor, usually a boy, stood precariously on the outside step and hung on grimly to the handrail as the bus lunged forwards over somewhat uneven road surfaces. It was not until the 'Naughty Nineties' that crews appeared in military styled uniforms and the efficient ticket issue by means of the famous Bell Punch and voluminous ticket rack were adopted on anything like a universal basis.

The horse-bus held supreme sway until well into the reign of Edward VII, and it was only with the appearance of such successful motorbuses as the Milnes-Daimler and the Straker-Squire, and steam buses like the Clarkson 'Chelmsford' that the swift decline in the fleets of horse-drawn vehicles began. Swift it was, for the last horse-bus ran in London on the eve of the First World War, although such buses were crossing the High Level Bridge at Newcastle-upon-Tyne until 1931. The last regular horse-bus route in Britain was between Chessington South railway station and Chessington Zoo, and this ended on 30th September 1948, when ex-Star Omnibus Company Nos. 2938 and 5074 were withdrawn from service as no longer fit for licensing.

Less than four years after Shillibeer's horse-buses began to frequent the streets of London, on 22nd April 1833 Walter Hancock of Stratford introduced his *The Enterprise* on to the same route to the Bank. For a fortnight this mechanical marvel was a serious competitor with its fourteen-seat body, powered by a steam engine. Then it was withdrawn for technical reasons, but was soon replaced by the *Autopsy,* which had first been tried out on the Finsbury to Pentonville route. By 1836 *Autopsy* had been joined by two more Hancock steamers, named *Era* (18-seater) and *Automaton* (22-seater). Nevertheless these were not the first steam buses to run in Britain, for Hancock's great rival, Goldworthy Gurney, had started a service between Cheltenham and Gloucester in February 1831. Four times each day until that June a steam drag pulled a trailer over the nine miles separating the two towns. Two years later Maudslay and

Field constructed an improved version of the Gurney drag for their London to Greenwich route.

That same year a Scot, John Scott Russell, began to run steam buses of his own design over this east London route, before trying out one of his 26-seaters on his native Glasgow to Paisley run (7 miles).

A generation was to elapse before the next series of steam buses took to the road, and then it was to be on the other side of Scotland, where the road from Edinburgh to Leith seemed to carry considerable traffic. In June 1870 R. W. Thomson introduced a 6 h.p. steam tractor that towed a rubber-tyred trailer bearing up to 65 passengers. Later that year this was joined by Andrew Nairn's 8 h.p. three-wheeled bus, with a seating capacity of fifty. Two years later Leonard Todd went one better with a four-wheeler capable of transporting seventy people at one go. Thereafter comes another interregnum when steam appears to vanish from the scene.

The next group of steam buses made their debut in 1897, when the Lifu *Pioneer* appeared on the streets of London for a short while, before it was sold to the Mansfield Motor Car Co. A second Lifu worked in Edinburgh between 1898 and 1901, whilst others were operating in east Kent. Based on a lorry chassis the Gillett steam bus of 1899 (plate 3) was tried experimentally as a 24-seater by the Motor Omnibus Syndicate in the London area, whilst in 1902 the capital witnessed another steam vehicle on trial: the Thornycroft, which carried 36 passengers. All these buses were notable for their tall chimneys that pierced the canopy that covered the upper deck.

It was at Eastbourne in the spring of 1903 that the really successful steam bus began to work reliably. This was a Clarkson, and soon similar single-deckers were to be found on stage carriage routes at Torquay, Worthing and Bridgnorth, in the last-mentioned case being employed by the GWR. In October 1904 the London Road Car Company put their seal on its acceptability by placing a Clarkson into service, following this by buying a double-decked version in 1905. The heyday of the steam bus was between 1907 and 1909, when not only did Clarksons run on LRCC and National Steam Car Company routes, but a rival Darracq-Serpollet with a flash type generator-boiler also appeared in fair numbers in the ranks of the Metropolitan Steam Omnibus Company. Nevertheless, by the outbreak of the First World War the demise of the steam bus had occurred, and so far no fourth generation has come off the drawing-board, although with the current threat of petrol and diesel pollution, they may yet be seen in our cities again before long.

If the steamer was not the answer to the outmoded horse-bus, perhaps an electric bus would succeed? Indeed as early as January 1889 a small electrically powered bus was working in London, built by the Ward Electrical Car Company. In 1891 Bersey ran a 26-seater electric battery bus experimentally between Victoria and Charing Cross. Due to the excessive weight of accumulators such vehicles could only move rather slowly. In 1906 the formation of the London Electrobus Company heralded a new era for such electric traction. By 1908 fourteen of these double-deckers were working the Brondesbury to Law Courts, and Earls Court to Liverpool Street routes, but two years later they were withdrawn and most of them were sold to the Brighton, Hove and Preston United Omnibus Company, who used them for a further six years.

Just about the time they were being scrapped the much smaller Edison battery bus came into its own in war-stricken Britain, now very short of petrol supplies. Southend-on-Sea Corporation seems to have been the first to try out such a vehicle, HJ 34 arriving in 1914. The next year saw four being used by West Bromwich Corporation, and next year Lancaster Corporation took delivery of the first of five such buses. Finally at the end of the war Derby Corporation tried out a pair of Edisons. These single-deckers sat between 22 and 25 passengers apiece. Their main snag seems to have been the five hours needed to recharge the batteries each day.

In November 1907 the following extract appeared in a Brighton newspaper:

> 'The bus companies have put upon the road huge machines which have polluted the atmosphere with asphyxiating odours, filled the air with insanitary particles, created so much vibration that the premises have appeared to be experiencing perpetual earth tremours, made such an irritating whirling noise that tradesmen have had to shut their doors in order to hear customers speak, driven carriage people clean out of the street, and freely bespattered with foul oily mud those pedestrians who braved the terrors of the pavements.'

A strong indictment of the infant motorbus, that was unknown a decade previously! By 1898 'motor cars' were acting as public service vehicles between Torquay and Paignton. By the end of that year the Hon. C. S. Rolls was trying out an imported 12 h.p. Cannstatt-Daimler single-decker bus, although that very summer F. E. Barton had run a motorbus service at Blackpool. Dr. E. M. Hailey and Mr. W. Carlisle, M.P. had begun a motorbus route twixt Newport Pagnell and Olney using a Daimler. In 1899 an English Daimler of 6 h.p. was to be found plying between Penzance railway station and Marazion.

In spite of the fact that unlikely places such as Kilmarnock, Llandudno and Mablethorpe had already experienced the delights (?) and novelty of riding in a motorbus before 1899, it was on 9th October of that year that Londoners had their first similar opportunities, when a German-built Daimler double-decker running on steel tyres was put into service by the Motor Traction Company between Kensington and Victoria. However, the real breakthrough appears to have happened on 26th November 1902 when the London Motor Omnibus Syndicate placed into service some twelve-seater Scott-Stirlings on their Oxford Circus to Cricklewood route. Two years later Thomas Tilling bought their first motorbus, a 24 h.p. Milnes-Daimler registered A 6934. Birch Bros. followed suit, and next spring saw this type of bus entering the ranks of the London Motor Omnibus Company, to be followed in its turn by the mighty London General Omnibus Company two months later.

Meanwhile Southampton Corporation had become the first municipality to operate a motorbus route, when from 5th August until 20th December 1901 they ran *hired* vehicles between the Clock Tower and Northam. Then on 12th April 1903 Eastbourne Corporation became the world's first local authority to actually *own* the motorbuses that they ran. Again the highly successful Milnes-Daimlers were chosen to start the services from the Railway Station to Meads.

A parallel development of the use of the motorbus started at the turn of the century, when some of the railway companies began to supplement their country services with 'feeder' bus routes. Amongst the leaders of this movement was the GWR, who inaugurated their entrance into the bus industry with a route between Helston and The Lizard on 17th August 1903.

A poem in the *Daily Chronicle* in Edwardian times had this verse:

Hurrah for the jolt of the 'Thunderbolt',
And the crunch of breaking teeth,
The sudden pause of the iron claws
As the driver dives beneath;
O, who would be in a storm at sea
Who might for a penny thus

Enjoy the pitch of the monster which
We christened the motorbus?

However, about that time there appeared upon the scene the first of a series of production models of the so-called 'petrol-electric' bus that aimed to combine the silent approach of the electric battery bus with the speed of the petrol-engined bus. Although an imported American Fischer petrol-electric double-decker of formidable proportions had been tried out by the LGOC in 1903, the first successful vehicle seems to have been 'L'Auto-Mixte' produced by Messrs. Pieper of Liège, whose British agents were Messrs. Johnston and Phillips of Charlton, Kent. The *Commercial Motor* for 1st March 1906 describes the vehicle in these words:

'The motive power is derived from a petrol engine in conjunction with an electric motor. Transmission is by an electric clutch, and a cardan shaft to the back axle, which carries the differential gearing. No gear box is used for the different speeds.'

In January 1908 the first Hallford-Stevens petrol-electric double-decker appeared, which found favour with the Brighton, Hove and Preston United Omnibus Company, perhaps to combat the local criticism mentioned earlier. It was the placing into service of the first Tilling-Stevens TTA1 petrol-electric by Thomas Tilling in 1911 that opened up a bright future for this type of vehicle (plate 5). In turn over the next seventeen years it found favour in many fleets, including those of Birmingham Corporation, Walsall Corporation and Southdown Motor Services. A six-wheeled version (the TS15) was tried out by Wolverhampton Corporation as late as 1928.

In 1910 mass production techniques began to be applied to the bus industry. Following the successful trials with London General's experimental X1-61 the previous year, their Walthamstow factory (later run under a separate company, AEC) started to turn out the first of almost four thousand of the famous 'B' class double-deckers and single-deckers, many of which served as troop transports in the First World War.

The body of the 'B' still looked as if it belonged to the horse-bus era, and although the seating had been increased to 34, this was still inadequate. So in 1919, with the need to replenish the depleted ranks of London buses, the AEC 'K' was built, seating 46 in a wider, lower body. Three years later the AEC 'S' came on to the scene, being larger still and seating 54. Its total overall length was 24 feet 7 inches and it was 7 feet 1 inch wide. Next on London's streets came NS 1-2387 between 1923 and 1928. During their delivery two important stages were reached, namely the first pneumatic-tyred double-decker to run regularly in the capital, and the first there to have roofs and windows on the upper deck. Nevertheless Widnes Corporation had placed their first covered double-deckers into service as early as 1909 (Commers registered B 2163-6).

1927 marks a turning point in the history of bus development in this country for it heralded in the first really viable six-cylinder double-decker bus, the famous Leyland 'Titan', 25 feet long and seating between 48 and 51 passengers in much more comfort than had hitherto been possible. Two years later it was joined by another highly successful double-decker: the AEC 'Regent', which was to be its rival for the next forty years!

During the decade 1925 to 1935 the problem of a limited length to bus bodies was partially got over by building six-wheel chassis. The most famous of these was probably the AEC 'Renown', which formed the basis of London General's LT class, which had seats for up to 66 (double-decker) or 35 (single-decker). Others in this field were the Guy BX and CX models, the Karrier WL6, the Leyland 'Titanic', the Maudslay 'Magna' and the Sunbeam 'Sikh'. Although the six-wheeled trolleybus became popular until after the Second World War, its motor-bus counterpart always remained as a comparatively small minority. In 1927 an ADC 802 six-wheeler was given a 104-seat body for transporting AEC workers between Walthamstow and that firm's new Southall factory!

In 1930 Leeds Corporation introduced the first double-decker bus to run regularly whilst powered by an oil engine. This was a Crossley 'Condor' fitted with a Gardner 6L2 engine of 8.4 litres, an engine originally designed for marine work! Other manufacturers followed suit during the Thirties, viz. Guy 'Arab' FD and Dennis 'Lance 2' (1933), AEC 'Regent' 0661 (1935), and Leyland 'Titan' TD5 and Maudslay 'Marathon' ML5 (1937).

On the single-decker front over this period between the wars there had been phenomenal success with the Leyland 'Lion' and 'Tiger' and the AEC 'Regal'. Experiments were carried out to reposition the engine so that more passengers could be seated within a vehicle of the same dimensions. London Transport's Q1-238 had their AEC engines placed on the offside behind the front axle, which enabled their 27-foot long bodies to seat 37 passengers. (Incidentally Q2-5 and Q188 were double-deckers.) Another attempt was tried out by Northern General with their SE4 and SE6 models, which also had side-positioned AEC engines. On the other hand in 1938 Shelvoke and Drewry sold two rear-engined 'Freighters' to Southdown for service in Worthing. Midland Red carried out experiments with their S.O.S. 'REC' rear-engined single-decker No. 1591 (BHA 1) two years previously, and followed this up with three more similar vehicles (1942-4, CHA 1-3).

During the 1930s many smaller towns and a few large cities such as Derby, Norwich, Nottingham, Portsmouth and Swansea closed down their tramway systems. In some cases these were replaced partially by trolleybuses, but in many cases motorbuses were substituted.

Following the First World War many members of the A.S.C. returning home with thousands of miles of commercial driving under their belt, began to run country bus routes, or else compete with the established operators in towns as 'pirates'. This led to a cut-price fares war and much dangerous driving to get their passengers to the terminus first. As from the passing of the Road Transport Act of 1930 with its stringent rules on licensing stage carriage routes all these worst aspects of private enterprise were brought under control.

After Dunkirk in June 1940 many routes were withdrawn or considerably curtailed; buses were commandeered by the War Department; vehicle manufacturers had to turn their attention to war production, and for a short time all production on new buses was halted. Then in 1942 was born the 'utility' bus with its angular lines, its grey livery and its wooden seats. Operators had to queue up (as their passengers were now lawfully commanded to do at bus stops) for the comparatively limited numbers of Guy 'Arabs' and Bedford OWBs that came off the assembly lines at Wolverhampton and Luton respectively.

In the period since V. J. Day in 1945 all but one of the 37 remaining tramway systems in Britain have become defunct, and all the 34 outstanding trolleybus networks, so that by 1971 the motorbus reigned supreme, although controlling a market that had shrunk annually since its peak in 1948-51. Between 1933 and 1946 the legal length of a two-axle double-decker had been 26 feet. From 1946 until 1954 it stood at 27 feet. In that latter year it jumped to 30 feet. Since 1966 it has been raised to 36 feet, although very few double-deckers over 34 feet in length have taken to the roads. In the case of single-deckers, their lengths have progressed similarly until they now stand at 12 metres (just short of 40 feet), although there have been experimental vehicles as long as 45 feet. Seating capacity has, of course, kept pace with these improvements, so that there are now 82-seat double-deckers and 60-seat single-deckers in existence in Britain.

Under-floor engined single-deckers replaced, by and large, the front engined vehicle with the arrival on to the transport scene of the Bristol LS and the Leyland 'Royal Tiger' in 1950, followed by the Atkinson 'Alpha' (1952) and the AEC 'Reliance' (1953). The next generation of single-deckers were to have their engines at the rear of the chassis, starting with the Bristol RE in 1962, followed by the Daimler 'Roadliner' and the Leyland 'Panther' (1964), and the AEC 'Swift' (1966). Nevertheless, it had been the double-deckers that had led the way this time, with the Leyland 'Atlantean' appearing as early as 1958 and the Daimler 'Fleetline' two years later, with the Bristol VR not making its debut until 1966. Midland Red did try out a pair of their revolutionary D10 under-floor engined double-deckers in 1959/61, but Nos. 4943/4 (KHA 943/4) were not followed by any production models.

Although some single-decker bus routes have always been one-man operated, 15th June 1966 is a landmark in such economy service, for on that date Brighton Corporation introduced their first one-man operated double-decker (a Leyland 'Titan' PD2, No. 23, 23 ACD) on to circular route 26A/46A in that seaside resort, to be followed a fortnight later by similar operation by Great Yarmouth Corporation. Manchester and Liverpool Corporations were quick to grasp the advantages of such workings, and on 2nd January 1971 London Transport converted routes 95 and 220 to one-man operation with their new 'Londoner' class of Daimler 'Fleetlines'. Express urban flat-fare operation using one-man buses can really be dated to 8th April 1966 when London Transport introduced its first 'Red Arrow' route between Victoria and Oxford Street (500) using AEC 'Merlins'.

3. THE DEVELOPMENT OF THE MOTOR COACH

The modern motor coach has its origins in the nineteenth century horse-drawn char-a-banc, with its rows of bench seats facing frontwards, and often fixed to a sloping floor so that each row of passengers could see over the heads of those sitting in front of them (Edwardian ladies' hats permitting!). Usually they were drawn by two horses, and took the town workers for jaunts into the countryside or to the seaside. They also plied for custom along the promenades of the Victorian watering places for the further enjoyment of holidaymakers. Many employers gave their workmen an annual treat in the form of an outing in privately hired 'charas'.

Similar in function to this vehicle was the wagonette, in which passengers sat on seats along the side of the body facing inwards towards one another. In Kingston-upon-Hull wagonettes seating ten passengers and drawn by a single horse began to appear on the streets of that port in the 1880s, and they became so popular that by the summer of 1899 no less than 410 were licensed to operate on the city streets. Although with the advent of electric trams they declined in numbers there were still as many as 93 operating at the outbreak of the First World War. The motorised wagonette, first produced by Daimler and shortly afterwards by Albion, started off the career of the motor coach. Thomas Barton began to operate such a motorised wagonette at Mablethorpe in 1898, and later ran excursions with one from Weston-super-Mare to Cheddar Gorge and other West Country beauty spots.

It was really the coming on to the scene of the reliable Milnes-Daimler 24 h.p. in 1904 that revolutionised the chara. By 1906 the Isle of Wight Express Motor Syndicate were operating two 30 h.p. versions of this vehicle for circular tours based on Ryde and travelling via Sandown and Shanklin. Further along the South Coast the Worthing Motor Omnibus Company in 1904 had invested in three Milnes-Daimlers with Harrington 25-seat chara bodies, and used CD 336/8/9 for their route along the coastal road to Brighton. Another early success was Durham-Churchill, who turned out large charas seating up to thirty excursionists, and smaller ones with room on their benches for only sixteen travellers. From 1907 another competitor, who was to make a great impact on the excursion scene, began to market from its Luton headquarters —Commercial Cars (better known as just 'Commer').

By the 1912 Scottish Show Albion were exhibiting a 32 h.p. chara for Largs Coast Service which had a so-called 'torpedo' body (plate 6) that sat 25 tourists. This was a roughly streamlined body with a central gangway, which could be filled with five tip-up seats. Side windows were provided for winter use, whilst roller curtains were a summer alternative. Charas were beginning to appear which had separate doors for each bench. In other cases old-style bodies still found their uses, especially when they were detachable, as with a Lacre 30 h.p. by Mr. F. Didham, a wholesale dairyman of Bristol, who advertised 'When not engaged in transport of milk, we fit char-a-banc bodies'. By 1914 extended tours lasting up to a week were starting to attract the more affluent clientele.

After the First World War express coach services between provincial towns and London began to attract custom away from the railways, and this became more successful after they had proved their worth during the General Strike of May 1926. The advent of the six-cylinder petrol engine gave motor coaches the extra power needed to compete on more even terms with the steam express train, whilst the employment of pneumatic tyres from the mid-1920s onwards gave as smooth a ride over the newly tarmacked main roads as could be achieved over the jointed main line rails. Some firms concentrated on this market. One interesting case was that of Gilfords (plate 14), who fitted American Lycoming engines on to British built Garford chassis, and then built their own bodies; although at the 1927 Olympia Show they did exhibit one of their new LL166 models with a Strachan and Brown body which had built into it both a toilet and a kitchen; facilities that have only become more common practice with the 'Gay Hostess' double-deck coaches of Ribble during the 1960s! Some operators were formed specifically to run these express coach routes, one of the most successful and famous being Black and White Motorways of Cheltenham.

At transport rallies to-day can sometimes be seen a small yellow and red coach, which in July 1931 created a coaching revolution. TM 9547 bears the Bedford chassis No. 1000001, and was the very first coach to emerge from this American firm's Luton factory. From the initial batch of 102 of the fourteen-seat WHB model evolved the much more numerous WLB, WTB, OB, SB, VAL and VAM models that have brought modern luxury coaches within the pocket of small operators and have in some cases been sold and resold, running regularly for two decades or more.

The opening of the M1 motorway in 1958 led to a new era for the express motor coach. Midland Red built some special vehicles for their Birmingham—London and Coventry—London routes that sped along the new artery at speeds of up to 85 m.p.h. Turbo-charged 8-litre under-floor engines powered the CM5 class (37 seats) and CM5T class (34 seats with toilet/hand basin compartment). However, speed was not the sole criterion for this new generation of vehicles. There was the safety aspect. Back in 1937 Leyland developed a chassis with twin front steering axles and named the 'Gnu', but very few were ever built. It was too in advance of its time to succeed, and it was left to Bedfords in 1962 to begin to mass-produce the first popular twin front axle coach, the VAL14, to be replaced in 1968 by the more powerful VAL70 version. The idea was that if one of the front tyres burst at speed, then there were sufficient other tyres strategically placed to avoid a disaster.

We must not forget the double-decker coach either. In 1931 Green Line introduced their first such vehicle in the form of AEC 'Renown' LT 1137 (GP 3456), but it was not until 1949 that the second such coach was tried out: AEC 'Regent' RTC 1 (FXT 272), seating 46 passengers, compared with the 56 it could seat in its former state as ordinary bus RT 97. The next experimental coach for Green Line came in 1956 with CRL 4 (SLT 59), and later renumbered as RMC 4. This AEC—Park Royal 'Routemaster' sat 57 passengers, and was the prototype for the first production double-decker coaches for London Transport, RMC 1453-1520. Later some longer 65 seat 'Routemasters' were brought into service as RCL 2216-2260. In 1959 Ribble and their subsidiary Standerwick introduced Leyland 'Atlanteans' with only sixteen passengers seated in the lower saloon (which also contained the buffet bar and toilets) and 34 in the upper saloon. These 'Gay Hostesses' operated down the M6 and M1 between Lancashire and London. A prototype replacement appeared in 1968, a Bristol VRLL with a sixty-seat body, and the production version began to enter service in 1970. These have twin doors, whereas their predecessors had only a front entrance. One of the ousted coaches (NRN 606) has had its upper deck remodelled, and is now run jointly by Samuelsons and Lyons as the 'Upper Crust' mobile restaurant, giving diners a tour of the West End during a meal.

There remains to tell of the short history of the half-decker, a hybrid vehicle of the 1930s and 1950s, in which the upper deck stretched only over the rear half of the vehicle. London Transport employed eight Leyland 'Cubs' with 18-seat half-deck coach bodies for their Inter-Station express routes in central London. Beneath the top deck was ample luggage space for rail travellers crossing from say Paddington to Victoria in blue and cream vehicles. In 1950 they were transferred to BEA, who later bought their own specially designed half-deckers in 1952/3. MLL 713-762 and NLP 636-650 based on AEC 'Regal IV' chassis and carrying 37 passengers along with their luggage, but unlike the 'Cubs' mentioned above they were not 'stepped' as far as the roof was concerned. In their turn they were replaced by 65 AEC 'Routemasters' seating 56 passengers and towing luggage trailers (KGJ 601-649 D and NMY 650-665 E) in 1966/7, along with eight 'Executive Express' coaches carrying 49 passengers and based on an AEC 'Reliance' chassis (KHM 1-8 D).

4. THE DEVELOPMENT OF THE TROLLEYBUS

Although the first trolleybus ran in Berlin as early as 1882, it was not until September 1909 that the British public had their first chance of seeing one of these electric vehicles in action. The Metropolitan Electric Tramways staged a demonstration in the yard of their Hendon depot in that month using a single-decked Railless Electric Traction vehicle. However, it was not until 24th June 1911 that the first British trolleybuses entered service, when simultaneously they began to operate in both Bradford and Leeds (plate 25). The initial vehicles had twin 20 h.p. electric motors of 525 volts and carried 28-seat bodies.

In 1912 systems were opened in Dundee (this one closed in 1914) and Rotherham, whilst the following two years saw trolleybuses operating in Aberdare, Keighley, Ramsbottom and Stockport. For a few weeks during the winter of 1914/15 trolleybuses operated in the Rhondda, and in 1915 they began to run between Mexborough and Swinton. The two main manufacturers in these early days were RET (see above) and Cedes-Stoll. In most systems the current was taken from the overhead wiring by means of a trolley wheel on the end of a long boom, but at Aberdare a different method was adopted. Here a four-wheeled trolley ran along the top of the single wire and this was connected to the vehicle by means of a flexible cable wound on to a drum under the bonnet. A plumb-bob suspended from the trolley helped to keep the cable under tension. A third method was employed by Stockport Corporation on their Brush-Cleveland trolleybuses and was known as the Lloyd-Kohler system. Here the two wires were placed one above the other, the negative being the uppermost one. A loose cable connected the trolley-wheel to the vehicle. As at Aberdare when trolleybuses met, they exchanged trolleys.

Bradford Corporation began to build their own trolleybuses in 1913, and seven years later they built a large double-decker which weighed almost 7½ tons and was 15 feet 4 inches tall. It was powered by a single 45 h.p. motor. There had been experimental Cedes-Stoll and RET double-decker trolleybuses before the First World War, but Bradford No. 521 (AK 9638) was the first to have a covered top deck. In 1922 that Corporation built a six-wheeler with twin steering axles.

New systems began opening directly the Armistice was signed, the first being on Tees-side (this also being the penultimate system to close, 1971), followed by York, Halifax and Birmingham. Although the latter always used double-deckers, most of the systems during the early 1920s were worked by single-deckers, New manufacturers of these vehicles appeared upon the scene: Associated Daimler, Garrett, Guy, Karrier, and Ransomes, Sims & Jefferies (RSJ), whilst we hear no more of Cedes-Stoll, and the last RETs were delivered to Nottingham Corporation in 1927. These were powered by twin English Electric 35 h.p. motors, but generally new models, such as the Garrett 'O', had a single 50 h.p. motor. Whereas many of the first trolleybuses had born a distinctive likeness to tramcars, so around 1930 they looked exactly like motorbuses in some instances. This was especially true in the case of the first Leylands bought by Birmingham Corporation, which, apart from their trolley booms, looked just like the Leyland 'Titan' TD1 motorbuses.

In the 1930s many more tram networks were swept away (e.g. Brighton, Bournemouth, Derby, Pontypridd and Portsmouth), being replaced by double-decker trolleybuses. These new markets brought back Daimlers on to the trolleybus scene in 1936 with a choice of their CTM4 four-wheeler and CTM6 six-wheeler models. That same year Crossleys followed suit with their TDD4 and TDD6 models. In 1931 one of the most famous names in trolleybus circles appeared: Sunbeam with their MS2 six-wheeler, which found immediate success with their local operators, Walsall Corporation and Wolverhampton Corporation, and later with Bournemouth Corporation. Again a four-wheeled model (the MF2) was marketed.

By 1936 a distinctive trolleybus design was emerging, with a fully-fronted body, and it was this shape that soon began to replace the huge London tramway network, until the advent of the Second World War halted its progress. AEC joined forces with Metro-Cammell Weymans to build many chassis-less trolleybuses for London Transport. These were of integral construction in which the chassis is part of the body and not constructed separately, as is the normal case.

During the Second World War only Karrier and Sunbeam were permitted to build trolleybuses, and these vehicles, designated W4s, were to strict austerity (or 'utility') regulations. Although after 1945 several trolleybus networks extended (e.g. Bradford, Huddersfield, Portsmouth, Reading, Tees-side) and one new system came into being (Glasgow Corporation's on 3rd April 1949), there were only four manufacturers to choose from. Of these Daimlers ceased to build any trolleybuses after 1950, whilst Crossleys were absorbed shortly after the end of the war by AEC, whose subsidiary company BUT had only one serious competitor left: Sunbeam. When the latter company built Bournemouth

Corporation Nos. 295-303 (295-303 LJ) in 1962, these MF2Bs were, in fact, the last trolleybuses ever to be built for the British market.

Trolleybus abandonment schemes began to grow in impetus as the 1960s proceeded, but even then it looked as if there would be at least three systems surviving until the 1980s, since they were buying up good second-hand vehicles from defunct networks. Thus Bradford purchased trolleybuses from Brighton, Darlington, Doncaster, Hastings, Llanelli, Mexborough and Swinton, Notts and Derby, and St. Helens, whilst Walsall took into its ranks those that had previously served in Grimsby and Cleethorpes, and Ipswich, whilst to Tees-side went ex-Reading trolleybuses. Then came three quick blows: the construction works on the M5 and M6 played havoc with Walsall's routes; the setting up of the County Borough of Tees-side brought about a change of policy, as did the arrival of a new general manager at Bradford. The final trolleybus routes (7 to Thornton and 8 to Duckworth Lane) ran for the last time on 26th March 1972.

However, using overhead equipment purchased from Bournemouth and Walsall a route is being laid out on the disused airfield at Sandtoft, near Doncaster, where trolleybuses, painstakingly restored, from many former systems should be giving rides to visitors by the summer of 1973. A similar venture is being carried out at Carlton Colville, near Lowestoft, jointly by the East Anglia Transport Society and the London Trolleybus Preservation Society.

5. SOME LEADING MAKES

AEC—LGOC 'B' class

It was on 12th August 1909 that Londoners living in the area of Walthamstow saw London General's new X1 (LC 7371), the prototype double-decker that was to lead the next year to the famous 'B' class, which quickly removed from the streets of London the motley collection of various makes that had vied with one another for supremacy during Edwardian times. These vehicles were powered by a 4-cylinder petrol engine that developed 35 b.h.p., but later with an increased bore this rating was raised to 42 b.h.p. The 'B' not only ousted earlier motorbuses, but also spelt the end of the horse-bus on the streets of the metropolis. It counts as Britain's first truly mass-produced bus, with 20 per week coming off the assembly lines by 1911. However, although mechanically the 'B' was a twentieth century product, its bodywork was of the nineteenth century, being high and narrow, like a horse-bus body, and only seating 34 passengers. At the outbreak of hostilities in 1914 the War Office ordered many 'B' chassis for troop transports and in their lorry form. In addition many of London General's fleet were commandeered to move the troops behind the Western Front. Some 'B' class chassis were given single-decked bodies.

In 1919 the buses that had failed to return from France and Belgium were replaced by the new AEC 'K' class, with a 28 h.p. engine. The 'K' was 6 inches nearer the ground than its predecessor, and slightly wider. Its redesigned body looked more like a motorbus, and it could seat 46 passengers. To get round the Metropolitan Police's weight regulations, 3-ply birch was employed instead of heavier timber. In 1922 came the even larger 'S' class powered by a 32 h.p. unit. This had a body 24 feet 7 inches long and 7 feet 1 inch wide, seating 54 passengers. Many of the 'S' class were single-deckers, some of which worked the famous route 108 through the Blackwall Tunnel. Finally, the following year AEC produced their 'NS' model with increased length (25 feet), increased width (7 feet 3½ inches) and increased engine power (35 h.p.), but with reduced seating (52), since more room was provided for each passenger. In 1925 the police at last relented their ban on roofs for double-deckers, whilst in 1928 the 'NS' was provided with pneumatic tyres as well.

Preserved examples

LA 9802 (LGOC B214); LA 9928 (LGOC B340); LN 4743 (LGOC B43); XC 8059 (LGOC K424); XL 8962 (LGOC S454); XM 7399 (LGOC S742); YR 3844 (LGOC NS 1995).

AEC 'Regent' Mark I

The first AEC 'Regent' appeared in 1929, designed as a rival to the already successful Leyland 'Titan' double-decker. It had a wheelbase of 15 feet 6½ inches and could take a 25 foot long body, which in those days would usually seat 48 to 51 passengers. The early 'Regents' were powered by an AEC 6-cylinder 6.1 litre petrol engine. In 1933 the wheelbase was increased by 8½ inches and the body length by 1 foot. In 1934 an optional 7.7 litre oil engine was available, although several operators preferred the more silent petrol engine, especially in quiet areas such as Cheltenham. London Transport based three large classes of double-deckers on the 'Regent' Mark I, the ST (Short Type with 25 foot long bodies), the STL (Short Type Long with 26 foot long bodies) (plate 15), and the RT, (Regent Type, the production of which stopped at RT 151 due to the outbreak of the war).

Preserved examples
AYV 651 (London Transport STL 314); BOR 766 (Gosport and Fareham 34); BOR 767 (Gosport and Fareham 35); CXX 457 (London Transport STL 1470); DLU 92 (London Transport STL 2093); DLU 240 (London Transport STL 1871); EGO 429 (London Transport STL 2377); EX 2877 (Great Yarmouth 30); FUF 63 (Brighton 63); FXT 219 (London Transport RT 44); FXT 229 London Transport RT 54); FXT 257 (London Transport RT 113); GJ 2098 (Tilling ST 922); GK 3192 (London General ST 821); JO 5403 (City of Oxford GA 16); OD 7489 (Devon General 202); OD 7497 (Devon General 210); OD 7500 (Devon General 213); RD 7127 (Reading 47); *SWU 222 F (Douglas 50).
*SWU 222 F was licensed as DMN 650 whilst on the Isle of Man.

AEC 'Regent' post-war marks

In 1945 AEC were permitted to resume the production of the 'Regent', and in the next three years nearly 700 of a new Mark II (plate 20) were built, with similar 7.7 litre engines to the pre-war Mark I model, and formed the basis for the final batch of London Transport's STL class, which spent their days at the Watford depot. Likewise London Transport continued their RT class with the Mark III, which had a 9.8 litre oil engine. A number of variants appeared on the market with a confusing array of codes such as the 6811A, 6813S, 9613E, etc. (see Kaye's *Buses and Trolleybuses Since 1945*, Blandford, 1968). In 1950 the length of some of these models was increased from 26 feet to 27 feet. In 1954 the Mark III was replaced by the Mark V, which soon became the standard AEC double-decker, 30 feet long and 8 feet wide. There was an experimental Mark IV that had an underfloor engine.

Preserved examples
AHC 442 (Eastbourne 42: III); BCP 671 (Halifax 277: III); BEN 177 (Bury 177: III); FAV 827 (Alexanders NRC 22: III); HAT 245 (Hull 245: II); HDK 835 (Rochdale 235: III); HGC 225 (London Transport STL 2692: II); HLW 159 (London Transport RT 172: III); HLW 178 (London Transport RT 191: III); HLX 146 (London Transport RT 329: III); HVO 937 (Mansfield District 126: II); JDN 668 (York Pullman 64: III); JV 9901 (Grimsby 81: III); JXC 194 (London Transport RT 1431: III); JXC 481 (London Transport RT 1173: III); KOD 585 (Devon General DR 585: III); KYY 520 (London Transport RLH 20: III); MRB 40 (Midland General 117: III); MTT 648 (Devon General DRD 648: III); MXX 223 (London Transport RLH 23: III); NTE 385 (Leigh 44: III); NTT 660 (Devon General DR 660: III); NTT 661 (Devon General DR 661: III); NTT 679 (Devon General DR 679: III); OLD 728 (London Transport RT 4508: III); ORR 140 (West Bridgford 21: III); XVO 329 (West Bridgford 31: V); ZH 3937 (Great Northern 438: III); 958 AJO (City of Oxford 958: V).

AEC 'Regal'

In 1929 AEC introduced their new single-decker chassis, which they called the 'Regal' (plate 15), as a counterpart to their 4-wheel double-decker, the 'Regent' and their 6-wheel double-decker, the 'Renown'. The Mark I 'Regal' had a rather long wheelbase of 17 feet, a common feature of such chassis at that period. It was powered by a 6-cylinder petrol engine. As a 30-seater saloon bus or coach it came at a time when many operators were beginning to develop a network of express services over the country, whilst London General urgently needed a replacement for its rather antiquated single-decked stock, hence the 'Regal' formed the basis for their T class that eventually reached 718 before hostilities halted temporarily its expansion further to T 793. These vehicles were the backbone of the surburban red bus routes and the Green line coach routes during the 1930s and 1940s. In 1933 the 'Regal' Mark I was lengthened from 26 feet to 27 feet 6 inches, its wheelbase growing correspondingly to 17 feet 6 inches. As from that time diesel engines began to be fitted to some Mark I 'Regals', there being a choice of an AEC 7.7 litre, or the more powerful AEC 8.8 litre unit. Between 1931 and 1936 a 4-cylinder version known as the 'Regal' 4 was produced in small numbers, and some of these survived in the active ranks of Gosport and Fareham Omnibus Company until 1968! As from 1936 a small oil engine of six cylinders was an option, but this Mark II model did not prove to be very popular. After the Second World War both Mark I and Mark II were manufactured for a short while, before they were ousted from the assembly lines by the Mark III in 1947 (plate 19). This was basically the 'Regent' Mark III double-decker chassis powered by an AEC 9.6 litre oil engine. Two years later a horizontally mounted form of this engine was developed, and by placing this amidships under the gangway floor the 'Regal' Mark IV was born. This enabled more passengers to be seated, and with an increase in the permitted length of a 2-axle single-decker to 30 feet this allowed 41 seated passengers to be conveyed.

Preserved examples

CLX 171 (London Transport T448: I); DOD 474 (Devon General SR 474: I); ELP 228 (London Transport T504: I); FV 4548 (Ribble 25: I); GK 5486 (Green Line T219: I); HLX 462 (London Transport T792: III); HUO 510 (Devon General SR 510: III); HUP 662 (Gillett Bros.: III); JF 2378 (Provincial: I); JVY 516 (York Pullman 65: III); JWO 355 (Bedwas and Machen 7: III); KKH 650 (Hull 155: III); LTA 628 (Devon General TCR 628: III); LTA 629 (Devon General TCR 629: III); LUO 593 (Devon General SR 593: III); LUO 595 (Devon General SR 595: III);

NJO 703 (City of Oxford 703: III); UU 6646 (London General T31: I); VO 5323 (Red Bus: I); WS 4482 (Alexanders: I); DMS 130 (Alexanders NA 104: III).

AEC 661T trolleybus series

In 1931 AEC began to manufacture the trolleybus version of their 'Regent' motorbus, and indeed the earliest 661Ts looked exactly like 'Regents' with twin trolley booms added to their roofs. However, by the time that the war halted their production the 661T had become very much a trolleybus designed in its own right (plate 26). The first 661Ts had an overall length of 25 feet and a wheelbase of 15 feet 6½ inches, and normally bore a 50 or 52 seat double-decked body. By 1939 56 passengers was the usual seating capacity of this model. The most common make of motor to be fitted to the 661Ts was English Electric, an 80 h.p. motor being the type involved. The AEC 663T trolleybus had appeared a year earlier than the 661T, and this was a 6-wheeler, being 27 feet long. London's first regular trolleybuses were of this model, and when London United Tramways placed them into service they were christened 'Diddlers', and they seated 56 passengers. Then in 1934 a lengthened version designated the 664T was placed on the market. This was 30 feet long and could seat up to 74 passengers, although 70 was the more usual number. Whereas the original batch of London 663Ts had English Electric 80 h.p. motors and the second batch BTH 82 h.p. motors, subsequent 661Ts and 664Ts had the stronger 95 h.p. motors.

Preserved examples

ARD 676 (Reading 113: 661T); CKG 193 (Cardiff 203: 664T); CPM 61 (Brighton, Hove and District 6340: 661T); CUL 260 (London Transport 260: 664T); FW 8990 (Cleethorpes 54: 661T); FZ 7883 (Belfast 98: 664T); HX 2756 (LUT 1: 663T); RV 4649 (Portsmouth 1: 661T).

Albion 'CX' series

Although the single-decker 'Valkyrie' can be traced back to 1931 and the double-decker 'Venturer' to 1933, the 'CX' series of these models began in 1938. Only one of the earlier sequence has survived, and this is a PW65 model, powered by an Albion 4-cylinder petrol engine and designed to take up to a 36-seat single-decker body. The later 'Valkyries' had a variety of engines such as the Albion 4-cylinder (CX9), the Gardner 5LW (CX11) and the Gardner 6LW or Albion EN242 6-cylinder 9.08 litre oil (CX13). The double-decker equivalent of the CX13 was designated the CX19 'Venturer'.

Science Museum

1. *A model of George Shillibeer's three-horse omnibus of 1829.*

2. *The first new motorbus bought by David MacBrayne Ltd. was this 1907 Albion 14-seater, which was chain driven.*

David MacBrayne Ltd.

H. Brearley

3. *A Gillett steam bus of the Edwardian era. Note the tall chimney penetrating the canopy over the 'knifeboard' seating arrangement on the top deck.*

4. *An early motor charabanc with chain drive, which operated on Guernsey. Note how the bench seats are on a sloping platform.*

A. E. Playden

W. J. Carman

5. *Birmingham Corporation No. 18, a 1912 vintage Tilling-Stevens TTA2 petrol-electric.*

J. Nickels

6. *A 'torpedo' styled charabanc body is fitted to DM 563, this Leyland 'S' type belonging to Brooke Bros. of Rhyl at the time of the First World War.*

7. *An interesting example of a single-decker bus of c. 1910 is this saloon run by the Belfast and County Down Railway Company.*

R. C. Ludgate

R. H. G. Simpson

8. *A 1927 Austin 22 h.p. 'toast-rack', UO 1477 belonged to the Sidmouth Motor Company and seated only thirteen.*

9. *With a display of working model trams on board at the Crich 1971 Transport Extravaganza is this 1929 vintage Dennis 'E', EA 4181, which was No. 32 in the fleet of West Bromwich Corporation.*

D. Kaye

R. H. G. Simpson

10. RU 8678 started life as a Leyland 'Lion' in the ranks of Hants and Dorset in 1929. It subsequently became a caravan . . .

11. . . . until enthusiasts restored it as a bus and entered it in the London to Brighton Commercial Vehicle Rally.

R. H. G. Simpson

Southdown M.S.

12. *During the peak period of the 1971 summer Southdown Motor Services brought out of retirement this 1929 Leyland 'Titan' TD1 to run along the Brighton and Hove sea fronts on a regular service.*

13. *Now preserved is ex-Belfast Corporation Dennis 'Lancet' No. 102 (CZ 7013) with a locally built Harkness body.*

W. H. Montgomery

R. H. G. Simpson

14. *Beautifully restored is this Gilford AS6 with a Buda engine. It belonged to Rivers of Ipswich in 1931 and had a 20-seat body.*

15. *An early Green line AEC 'Regal' (left), London Transport's STL 2093 (centre) and Lord Lonsdale's 20 h.p. Commer estate bus of 1909 (right) line up on Madeira Drive, Brighton, at the close of a rally.*

R. H. G. Simpson

R. H. G. Simpson

16. *London Transport's 1939 Leyland 'Cub' CR14 is the only preserved one with a rear mounted engine.*

17. *Delivered new to Bournemouth Corporation in 1939, FEL 216 is a Bedford WTB now in the safekeeping of the Poole and District Model Railway Society.*

R. H. G. Simpson

D. Kaye

18. WG 9833, seen at Crich in 1971, is a 1942 vintage Bedford OWB with a 1948 Duple body, now converted into a dormobile.

19. AY 101 started off life as JOD 621 in the fleet of Devon General, passing through the hands of Western Welsh, before being parked outside Riduna's depot in St. Annes, Alderney. It is a Duple bodied AEC 'Regal' III.

D. Kaye

D. Kaye

20. *A line up at Crich Quarry that includes Jersey Transport's Dennis 'Pax' No. 81, Kingston-upon-Hull Corporation's AEC 'Regent' II No. 245, and Aberdeen Corporation's Daimler CWA6 No. 155.*

21. *Converted into an open topper when it became No. 5995 in the ranks of Brighton, Hove and District, this Bristol K5G was previously on the city routes in Bristol.*

R. H. G. Simpson

R. H. G. Simpson

22. *The lifted bonnet exposes the Gardner 5LW engine of this Birkenhead Corporation Guy 'Arab' II. Although No. 242's chassis dates from 1943, the Massey body is ten years younger.*

23. *JGD 675 is a 1948 Foden PVD6 with a Scottish Aviation body that used to be No. 13 in the fleet of Garelochhead Coaches.*

R. H. G. Simpson

R. H. G. Simpson

24. *FBO 350 is a preserved example of a Davies bodied Dennis 'Lancet' J3 of 1950.*

25. *Leeds Corporation Railless Electric Traction trolleybus No. 501 was one of the first to enter public service in Britain in 1911.*

Leeds City Transport

E. Ogden

26. *On display at the Montagu Motor Museum at Beaulieu is Portsmouth Corporation's first trolleybus No. 201, an AEC 661T of 1934.*

27. *Originally in 1948 a 35-seat single-decker trolleybus working for Mexborough and Swinton Traction, FWX 912 became a 66-seat double-decker with Bradford Corporation in 1962. This Sunbeam F4 was at the Duckworth Lane terminus in October 1971.*

D. Kaye

R. N. Ashton

28. *The first open day at the Sandtoft Transport Centre, September 1971, and ex-Huddersfield Corporation Sunbeam S7 trolleybus No. 619 is taking fare-paying passengers on a circular trip using its batteries for power.*

E. Ogden

29. *A trio of South Lancs Transport 1933 vintage Guy BTX trolleybuses (Nos. 37, 35 and 33) lie mouldering at Atherton depot in 1958.*

30. *At the East Anglia Transport Museum at Carlton Colville, near Lowestoft, on 8th May 1971 ex-Ashton-under-Lyne No. 87 (a BUT 9612T with a rare Bond body), a vintage Thornycroft lorry and ex-Blackpool tram 159 were on working display for BBC cameras.*

London Trolleybus Preservation Society

When production was resumed after V. J. Day, the 'Venturer' was given the new Albion EN243 9.9 litre engine and called the CX37. The CX39 was the single-decker 'Valkyrie' produced in the post-war period, and differed little from the 'Venturer' in details. When the 'CX' series ceased to be built in 1953 Albion of Scotstoun, Glasgow, were already a subsidiary of Leyland Motors, and quickly losing their individual appeal, such as their distinctively shaped radiator.

Preserved examples

EGA 79 (Glasgow B92: CX37S); FTH 200 (West Wales: CX39N); FVA 854 (Highland Bus: CX39N); GWT 930 (South Yorkshire 61: CX13); HDG 448 (Cheltenham and District 72: CX19); JWR 875 (South Yorkshire 72: CX37); TWY 8 (South Yorkshire 81: CX37); WG 1448 (Alexander F55: PW65).

Bedford models of the 1930s

The first Bedford coach to be built in Britain entered service with J. Woodham of Melchbourne at the end of August 1931. This was one of 102 WHBs built. Their wheelbase was a mere 10 feet 11 inches and they normally carried a 14-seat body. The WHB was powered by a Bedford 3.18 litre 6-cylinder petrol engine. Between 1931 and 1935 Bedfords also built a larger model, the WLB, which had a wheelbase of 13 feet 1 inch and was suited to be fitted with a 20-seat body. A grand total of 1,431 WLBs were sold to British operators, mainly to the smaller firms. From 1935 until 1939 Bedfords concentrated on a larger version, the WTB (plate 17), which had an increased wheelbase of 13 feet 11 inches and could carry 26 passengers. As with the WLB a 27 h.p. Bedford petrol engine was the usual means of propulsion for the 2,556 of this model that found their way on to the home market. Most of these small Bedfords were employed as either excursion coaches in seaside resorts, or else by village proprietors for their market town routes. However, it is nice to think that two used by Bournemouth Corporation on their less well patronised local town routes have survived to show that the WTB had an urban potential that was not always obvious.

Preserved examples

AAF 66 (Greenslade: WLB); CDL 920 (Holmes, Cowes: WTB); CMG 30 (Garner: WLB); DDV 55 (Southern National 489: WTB); EAL 113 (Gash: WTB); FEL 216 (Bournemouth 13: WTB); FEL 218 (Bournemouth 15: WTB); GV 1173 (F. Cross: WLB); JT 8077 (South Dorset: WTB); MV 8996 (Howard: WLB); TM 9547 (Woodham: WHB); WS 5169 (WLB).

Bedford OB

During the summer of 1939 Bedfords introduced a new model capable of carrying 26 passengers and powered by a 28 h.p. petrol engine. Unfortunately production ceased due to the outbreak of the Second World War after only 73 OBs had come off the production line. The OB had a wheelbase of 14 feet 6 inches. None of the 52 OBs of this 1939 batch that were sold to the home market have survived. In 1942 permission was given to start manufacture of a wartime version of this chassis, designated the OWB (plate 18). Many of the 3,189 OWBs built in the next three years had 32-seat bus bodies with wooden slatted seats, wide destination boxes above the windscreen, and very angular looking 'utility' bodywork by a host of large and small coachbuilding firms. Subsequently some of these OWBs received newer post-war coach bodies, and therefore look identical to the later OBs. However, some of the austerity bodies continued in service in such places as the Isle of Man until as late as 1966. The production of a further 7,200 OBs for the home market began in 1946 and lasted until 1950, when the larger SB model replaced the OB. Many of the OBs received Duple bodywork, which has been common to the majority of Bedford coaches through the ages. Some OBs subsequent to their manufacture had their Bedford petrol engines replaced by Perkins P6 diesel units.

Preserved examples

BUX 608 (Whittle: OWB); CAW 360 (OWB); CFV 851 (OB); CTP 200 (Portsmouth 170: OWB); EUX 341 (T. Price: OB); FWW 596 (West Yorkshire CP1: OB); GDL 312 (Seaview Services: OB); GWF 358 (Connor and Graham: OB); JRR 114 (Barton 529: OB); KDD 866 (Moorland Heather: OB); KEL 679 (Hants and Dorset 687: OB); KJH 731 (Kirby: OB); LRB 750 (Booth and Fisher: OB); LRR 655 (Barton 594: OB); LTA 752 (Western National 1413: OB); NBB 171 (Tait: OB); NBH 941 (Rover Bus Service: OB); OPJ 200 (Walton-on-Thames Motors: OB); WG 9833 (Alexanders: OWB); SS 7486 (Stark B12: OB).

Bristol K series

The Bristol 'K' series had a long life, the first model (the K5G) (plate 21) coming into service in 1937, powered by the 7 litre Gardner 5LW engine. In the early years it normally bore a body measuring 26 feet by 7 feet 6 inches. As with other makes of chassis there was a break in production after 1941, but in 1944 this was resumed, but as the Bristol K6A, powered by an AEC 6-cylinder 7.7 litre oil engine. After the end of hostilities two further versions appeared: the K6G (with a Gardner 6LW engine) and the K6B (with a Bristol 8.1 litre unit). With the nationalisation of Bristol Motors in 1948 the 'K' could only thereafter be sold to other members of the British Transport Commission, which meant that members of the giant British Electric Traction (e.g. Maidstone and District, North Western Road Car) along with municipalities (e.g. Merthyr Tydfil, Rotherham) had to turn to other manufacturers to meet their needs. In 1950 two new versions appeared for BTC operators, namely the Bristols KS (27 feet long by 7 feet 6 inches wide) and the KSW (27 feet long by 8 feet wide). The last Ks came off the assembly lines in 1957, by which time most of the BTC members had been taking into their fleets the Bristol 'Lodekka' as a replacement.

Preserved examples

AJA 152 (North Western 432: K5G); AJN 825 (Westcliff-on-Sea: K5G); CAP 211 (Brighton, Hove and District 6356: K5G); CAP 234 (Brighton, Hove and District 6350: K5G); CWT 671 (West Yorkshire KDG 26: K5G); FAM 6 (Wilts and Dorset 289: K6B); FHT 112 (Bristol C3209: K5G); FKL 611 (Maidstone and District 273: K5G); FNY 933 (Pontypridd 40: K6A); FRP 692 (United Counties 692: KS5G); FRU 308 (Hants and Dorset TD 772: K6A); GHN 189 (United Automobile: K5G); GHT 124 (Bristol C3312: K5G); GKE 68 (Chatham and District 874: K5G); GLJ 964 (Hants and Dorset TD 787: K5G); GLJ 971 (Hants and Dorset TD 794: K5G); GLJ 986 (Hants and Dorset TD 809: K5G); HKE 867 (Maidstone and District DH 159: K6A); JDL 38 (Southern Vectis 764: KSW5G); JEL 249 (Hants and Dorset 1230: K6B); LTA 813 (Western National 994: KS5G); VNO 857 (Eastern National 1402: KSW5G); EJB 241 (Thames Valley 519: K6B); JRX 818 (Thames Valley 743: KSW6B); ONO 59 (Eastern National 4038: KSG).

Bristol L series

The Bristol L5G with its Gardner 5-cylinder 5LW engine first appeared in 1936 as a replacement for the earlier JO5G single-decker chassis. Until production temporarily ceased in 1941 both Tilling group operators, members of the BET group and municipalities bought the L5G for both town and country routes. Some found their way on to express coach services as well. Between 1946 and 1950 the basic 'L' chassis was designed for a 35-seat bus or coach of 27 foot length and being 7 feet 6 inches wide. As well as the 5LW engine, other alternatives were the fitting of a Bristol 6-cylinder AVW engine (the L6B model), an AEC 7.7 litre engine (the L6A model) and a Gardner 6LW engine (the L6G model). Between 1950 and 1952 two longer versions were placed into service, suitable for carrying 39 passengers in a body 30 feet long. The

LL was 7 feet 6 inches wide, but the LWL model was 8 feet broad. There was still a choice of Bristol or Gardner engines. The prototype Bristol LS appeared in 1950, but it was not until 1952 that this under-floor version of the L went into full production. Unlike the L, LL and LWL, the LS was of integral construction, i.e. the body was built at the same time as the chassis. The LS5G had as its power unit the horizontally mounted Gardner 5HLW, whilst the LS6G had the 6-cylinder version of this engine. By the time the LS ceased to be built in 1957, some 1,404 had entered service in Britain. Because it had an engine placed amidships under the flooring, the LS could carry up to 45 passengers in its bus form, without increasing the overall measurements of the LWL model.

Preserved examples

AJA 118 (North Western 364: L5G); AJA 132 (North Western 372: L5G); BOW 168 (Hants and Dorset TS 674: L5G); ETT 956 (Western National 262: L5G); FFW 830 (Lincolnshire 2020: L5G); FHN 833 (United Automobile BG147: L5G); FWX 802 (West Yorkshire 227: L6B); GAM 215 (Wilts and Dorset 296: L6B); HHN 202 (United Automobile DG216: L5G); HOD 30 (Royal Blue 1228: L6A); JUO 983 (Royal Blue 1218: L6B); KNO 603 (Eastern National 3900: L5G); LFM 731 (Crosville SLG 150: LL5G); LTA 722 (Western National 1613: LWL5G); LTA 729 (Royal Blue 1250: L6B); LTA 805 (Western National 1646: LWL6B); LTA 958 (Southern National 1324: LL6B); OTT 85 (Southern National 1376: LS6G); JRU 67 (Hants and Dorset 664: LL6A).

British United Traction trolleybuses

After the Second World War AEC, who had been producing the 661T and 664T trolleybuses in the 1930s and Leylands, who had manufactured their TB series of trolleybuses, amalgamated their interests in this field to make electric passenger vehicles under the subsidiary British United Traction (BUT). From 1948 to 1951 BUT built for the home market 136 of their 4-wheel 9611T model, 26 feet long and normally 7 feet 6 inches wide, capable of carrying double-deck bodies seating 54 or 56 passengers. There was much of the appearance of the old 661T in the 9611T, as the two chosen numbers hint at. This model was replaced by the 9612T (plate 30) in 1954, and Manchester Corporation and Ashton-under-Lyne Corporation (who operated a joint service) purchased the only seventy of this version that found a buyer in Britain. In 1956 BUT introduced their 9613T model, and all 90 that were built were sold to Glasgow Corporation. The 9612T was 27 feet long, whilst the 9613T was 30 feet in length. The former sat 60 or 61 passengers, whilst the latter could cope with 10 more. The last 9613T went into service at the close of 1958. The electric motors for this series of four wheelers varied from 95 h.p. up to 125 h.p. The 6-wheeled BUT 9641T flourished between 1948 and 1956, during which time almost 500 were built. The 9641T was 30 feet long and had a wheelbase of 18 feet 5 inches (2 feet 1 inch longer than that of the 9612T). Although the majority of the 9641Ts were given double-decker bodies, Cardiff Corporation did have some with 38-seat dual entrance /exit single-decker bodies for use on their Bute Street route, where a low railway bridge had to be negotiated. These received the nick-name 'Doodlebugs'. London Transport replaced their 'Diddlers' with 9641Ts powered by 120 h.p. Metrovick motors. The smallest batch of BUT models to be produced was for the RETB1, all 21 entering the ranks of Glasgow Corporation between 1951 and 1953. No. TBS1 was 33 feet long and was powered by a Metrovick 115 h.p. motor, Nos. TBS2-11 were 35 feet long and had 120 h.p. English Electric motors, whilst the remainder were 34 feet 6 inches long and had 125 h.p. Metrovick motors. All had single-deck bodies which seated either 36 passengers (central entrance) or 50 passengers (front entrance).

Preserved examples

*BDJ 83 (St. Helens 383: 9611T); BDJ 87 (St. Helens 387: 9611T); DBO 475 (Cardiff 215: 9641T); DRD 130 (Reading 144: 9611T); *EKU 743 (Bradford 743: 9611T); *EKU 745 (Bradford 745: 9611T); EKU 746 (Bradford 746: 9611T); ERV 313 (Portsmouth 313: 9611T); *FKU 758 (Bradford 758: 9611T); FYS 839 (Glasgow TB 78: 9613T); FYS 988 (Glasgow TBS 13: RETB1); FYS 996 (Glasgow TBS 21: RETB1); GFU 692 (Cleethorpes 59: 9611T); HYM 768 (London Transport 1768: 9641T); KBO 961 (Cardiff 243: 9641T); KLJ 346 (Bournemouth 246: 9641T); KTV 493 (Nottingham 493: 9611T); KTV 502 (Nottingham 502: 9641T); TV 506 (Nottingham 506: 9641T); KTV 578 (Nottingham 578: 9641T); LCD 52 (Brighton 52: 9611T); *LHN 781 (Darlington 69: 9611T); *LHN 783 (Darlington 71: 9611T); LHN 784 (Darlington 72: 9611T); *LHN 785 (Darlington 73: 9611T); NBB 628 (Newcastle-upon-Tyne 628: 9641T); NNU 234 (Notts and Derby 353: 9611T); NNU 238 (Notts and Derby 357: 9611T); ONE 744 (Manchester 1344: 9612T); YTE 826 (Ashton-under-Lyne 87: 9612T).

*At time of writing these were expected to be preserved.

Crossley 42 series

Although the Crossley 42 was planned for 1942, wartime conditions precluded its full-scale production until 1946. The 42 series of chassis were 7 feet 6 inches wide and had a wheelbase of either 16 feet 7½ inches (double-decker version) or 17 feet 7 inches (single-decker model). Both were powered by the Crossley 6-cylinder HOE7 engine of 8.6 litres. Some forms of the chassis were built to an 8-foot width (e.g. the 42/4 and the 42/8). The DD42/6 version was designed specifically for Birmingham Corporation, who actually preferred the ordinary production model, the DD42/7, after all. The difference between the DD42/5 and the DD42/7 lies in the improvements carried out to the Crossley oil engine involved. The final vehicles of the 42 series came into service in 1952, and were the last distinctive product from the Crossley works at Stockport.

Preserved examples

EBO 900 (Cardiff 46: DD42/5); EDB 575 (Stockport 321: DD42/7); ERD 154 (Reading 85: DD42/7); FBU 827 (Oldham 368: DD42/8); GDL 33 (Nash: SD42/7); GWM 816 (Southport 116: SD42/7); HET 513 (Rotherham 213: DD42/8); JOJ 489 (Birmingham 2489: DD42/7); NRA 717 (Chesterfield 17: SD42/7).

Daimler COG5 and its successors

In 1934 Daimlers introduced their successful double-decker the COG5, which was powered by a Gardner 5LW engine, although some Scottish operators took delivery of COG6s with Gardner 6LW units instead. Birmingham Corporation were especially keen on the COG5, which carried between 50 and 54 passengers. Its counterpart for single-deck work was the COG5-40, which in spite of the last part of its designation usually seated 38. Production of the COG series ceased in 1941, and two years later it re-emerged as the CWG5 with aluminium parts replaced by steel and cast iron. This was soon followed by the more popular CWA6 (plate 20), powered by an AEC 7.7 litre engine. Early in 1945 Daimlers began to put into some of the chassis being assembled their own 6-cylinder 8.60 litre engine, and these were designated as CWD6s. London Transport's D class consisted of a mixture of CWA6s and CWD6s. After the end of World War II Daimlers reverted to pre-war standards for their chassis, and so was born the CVG6 with its Gardner 6LW engine. Others of the CV series were fitted with AEC 7.7 litre engines (CVA6s) or Daimler's own CD650 10.6 litre engine (CDV6s). In 1956 a 30-foot long version was brought out, called the CVG6—30. This latter model was sometimes powered by a Gardner 10.45 litre 6LX engine, instead of the more normal 8.4 litre 6LW unit. Production of the CV series finally ceased in the 1960s.

Preserved examples
ACH 627 (Derby 27: CVD6); BMS 405 (Midland Alexanders D10: CVD6); BMS 414 (Midland Alexanders D19: CVD6); BMS 415 (Midland Alexanders D20: CVD6); BRS 37 (Aberdeen 155: CWA6); CCX 777 (Huddersfield 217: CWA6); CVP 207 (Birmingham 1107: COG5); FEA 156 (West Bromwich 156: CVG6); FMN 955 (Douglas 52: CWA6); FOP 429 (Birmingham 1429: CWA6); FSC 182 (Edinburgh 135: CVG6); GKV 94 (Coventry 94: CVA6); GNN 410 (West Bridgford 25: CWA6); GNU 750 (Tailby and George Dr5: COG5-40); GYE 98 (London Transport D93: CWA6); GYG 205 (Rossie: CVD6); GZ 1882 (Belfast 214: CWA6); JFJ 606 (Exeter 43: CVD6); JFJ 873 (Exeter 173: CVD6); JND 728 (Manchester 4127: CVG6); OHK 432 (Colchester 4: CVD6); ORB 277 (Tailby and George CVD6).

Dennis 'Ace' and 'Mace'

Known as the 'Flying Pig', the Dennis 'Ace' gained this nickname due to the snout-like appearance of its bonnet that protruded from the front axle that was set well back in order to ensure as small a turning circle as possible. This made the 'Ace' ideal for rural routes where there might be very limited room for manoeuvering at the terminus. The 'Ace' saw the light of day in 1934 and is what is termed a 'normal' control vehicle (i.e. the driver sits *behind* the engine). In contrast its stable mate the 'Mace' was a similar size forward control model (i.e. the driver sat *beside* the engine). The different positioning of the engine resulted in two important features. Firstly the 'Mace' was the opposite in frontal appearance to the 'Ace' and was almost fully fronted. Secondly the 'Mace' was able to seat 26 passengers against 20 for the 'Ace'. In 1938/9 the 'Ace' was succeeded by the 'Pike' and the 'Mace' by the 'Falcon', the latter being able to increase the seating to up to 32. These Dennis models were amongst the last public service vehicles to be fitted with 4-cylinder petrol engines.

Preserved examples
BTA 59 (Southern National 668: Mace); CTW 210 (Eastern National 3614: Ace); CYF 163 (L.C.C.: Mace); ECV 412 (Pearce: Ace); FUF 181 (Southdown 81: Falcon); JG 4234 (East Kent: Ace).

Foden PVD6 model

Between 1947 and 1956 Fodens produced a double-decker chassis at their Sandbach (Cheshire) works. This found favour mainly in Cheshire, Staffordshire and Lancashire, where these distinctive fully fronted double-deckers could be seen running local routes or on cross-country journeys. The PVD6 (plate 23) was usually powered by the Gardner 6LW 8.4 litre engine which had to cope with the 600-foot climb up Mow Cop, immediately it left the factory for testing. The PVD6 was 27 feet long, the same length as its single-decked equivalent, the PVSC6, which was also driven by a Gardner 6LW unit, although a few had the smaller 5LW engine, and are thus designated PVSC5s. Again, a few PVSC chassis received a 2-stroke Foden FD6 engine, but operators interested in this kind of power unit seemed to favour the Commer 'Avenger' marks III and IV with their Rootes TS3 diesel. The 2-stroke seemed to be quite good along fairly flat routes, but found it tough going on steep hills.

Preserved examples

FDM 724 (Phillips: PVD6); JGD 675 (Garelochhead 13: PVD6); LMA 284 (PVSC6); MED 168 (Warrington 102: PVD6); ONW 2 (Ledgard: PVSC Two-stroke).

Ford model 'T'

One of the most famous models ever produced anywhere in the world was the Model 'T' Ford, that found favour with many a one-man operator immediately after the 1918 Armistice. Basically this lightweight could cope with a 14-seat body, which was sometimes home-made, as in the case of Fentiman of Seaton Ross. This operator would remove the body on some days so that BT 9420 became a flat platform lorry to cart his produce to Selby market. Other days it took passengers into York, Others, such as Wyatt of Yattendon, ran a 'T' lorry-bus, i.e. the vehicle's body could carry both people and goods at the same time. Some 'Ts' were given a chassis extension and as the 'TT' could carry 20 passengers as a result.

Preserved examples

BH 4081 (Wyatt: T); BT 9420 (Fentiman: T); DD 475 (Freeman: T); EP 1673 (T); KK 980 (Riddell: TT).

Guy 'Arab'

Since none of the Guy 'Arabs' manufactured between 1933 and 1941 have survived we will concentrate on the new version of this Wolverhampton built chassis that came on to the wartime scene in 1942 with the 'Arab' Mark I. This was a 26 foot long double-decker with a wheelbase of 16 feet 3 inches and had a chassis made of steel, which made the completed vehicle weigh in the region of 8 tons: about a ton more than in pre-war double-deckers. The engine used in the Mark I was the 5-cylinder Gardner 5LW of 7.0 litres, but after the first 500 were built, it was decided to equip future 'Arabs' with the more powerful 6-cylinder Gardner 6LW engine of 8.4 litres. The next 2,000 'Arabs' were designated Mark IIs (plate 22) and to cope with this larger engine they had to be 5 inches longer (indeed 5 inches beyond the maximum allowed by law at that time for 2-axle double-deckers). London Transport bought 435 of these 'Arabs' to form their G class. In 1946 the Mark III made its debut. This reverted to the lighter construction of pre-war models. Although the Gardner 5LW and 6LW units were the normal engines used, there were some notable exceptions. For example some of the Mark IIIs were given the powerful Meadows 10.35 litre engine (the 6DC630), including London Transport's G436. Lincoln Corporation had their No. 23 fitted with a locally built Ruston and Hornsby 8.6 litre air-cooled engine, whilst Gosport and Fareham tried out some 'Arabs' powered by German Deutz FGL514 air-cooled units. In answer to a request by Birmingham Corporation in 1949 in connection with their tramway abandonment scheme, Guys developed an 8-foot wide version, the Mark IV, which had other refinements such as flexible engine mountings and triple-servo vacuum brakes. Concealed radiators were an option on the Mark IV. In 1956 some 30-foot long Mark IVs were introduced on to the market, and when the frames of these were lowered to enable front entrances to be built in 1963 the 'Arab' had reached Mark V. Between 1951 and 1959 an under-floor engined single-deck version of the 'Arab', called the LUF was on sale.

Preserved examples

AWG 393 (Alexanders FRO 607: III); BG 8857 (Birkenhead 242: II); BMS 848 (Alexanders G78: III); CCX 801 (County Motors 70: II);; DFE 383 (Lincoln 23: III); DHR 192 (Swindon 51: I); EFN 182 (East Kent: III); EHO 228 (Gosport and Fareham 55: I); EHO 869 (Gosport and Fareham 57: II); EWO 467 (Red and White L 442: I); EXG 892 (Middlesbrough 92: IV); FA 9291 (Burton-on-Trent 62: III); FNY 663 (Pontypridd 37: II); HGC 130 (London Transport G351: II); HWO 342 (Red and White L 1749: III); JTA 314 (Devon General DG 314: II); JV 8699 (Grimsby 72: II); TFJ 808 (Exeter 50: IV).

Karrier/Sunbeam W4 trolleybus

From 1942 until 1945 Karrier (who had been taken over by Sunbeam) and its parent company were the sole manufacturers of trolleybuses in Britain. Their wartime model bore the designation W4, and was a 26 feet long, 7 feet 6 inches wide vehicle, which might bear either a Karrier (K in the list below) or a Sunbeam (S in the list below) maker's plate on its bodywork. The first of the W4s went to Bradford Corporation, and like most wartime double-decked vehicles had a body of 'utility' pattern seating 56 passengers. However, Darlington Corporation did have some W4s fitted with 33-seat central entrance single-deck bodies. One of these (No. 24) has survived, but as Bradford No. 785 and with a much later double-deck body. Many of the W4s were, in fact, rebodied after the war was over, and so rather conceal their austere origins. Normally the W4 was powered by one 80 h.p. motor, which might have been manufactured by GEC, English Electric or Metropolitan Vickers.

Preserved examples

BDY 809 (Hastings Tramways 34: S); CDT 636 (Doncaster 375: K); DUK 833 (Wolverhampton 433: S); GHN 403 (Darlington 24: K); GHN 574 (Darlington 20: K); GKP 511 (Maidstone 56: S); GTV 666 (Nottingham 466: K); HKR 11 (Maidstone 72: S); RC 8472 (Derby 172: S); RC 8475 (Derby 175: S).

Leyland 'Lion'

The earliest of the Leyland 'zoo' public service vehicles was the 'Lion' (plates 10 and 11) that roared into existence in 1925 with the sound of its 4-cylinder 5.1 litre petrol engine. The PLSC1 model was planned to seat 32, whilst the following year a slightly larger version (the PLSC3) came on the scene with the possibility of up to 36 seated passengers. Although many operators in the 1930s turned for their single-deckers to the 6-cylinder Leyland 'Tiger', the 'Lion' continued to be developed and sought after, particularly in the North. In 1929 a 4-cylinder version of the Leyland 'T' engine (that powered the 'Tiger' and the 'Titan') appeared, thus starting the LT series of 'Lions'. Throughout the 1930s each change in the chassis design of the 'Tiger and the 'Titan' was mirrored in a change in the 'Lion' of a similar nature. Progressively the wheelbase (and thus the overall chassis length) was lengthened, viz. 16 feet 7¾ inchcs (LT1), 17 feet 6 inches (LT3), 17 feet 7 inches (LT5A), 17 feet 8½ inches (LT9). As from the LT5 an optional 4-cylinder 5.7 litre oil engine was offered. As with its Leyland contemporaries, a suffix 'c' denotes a gearless version. Certain models (e.g. LT4, LT6 and LT9) appear to have gone mainly to Irish operators. After 1940 production ceased, and after the Second World War was not resumed since there seemed to be no market for 4-cylinder single-deckers seating nearly 40 passengers. The normal control equivalent of the PLSC1 was the PLC1 'Lioness' and of the LT1 the LTB1 'Lioness'.

Preserved examples
ATD 683 (Widnes 39: LT7); BR 7132 (Sunderland 2: LT1); BTB 928 (Lytham St. Annes 34: LT7c); BTF 24 (Lytham St. Annes 44: LT7c); DM 6228 (White Rose 7: LTB1); DV 7890 (Devon General 15: LT2); FV 6128 (Blackpool 128: LT7); J 4601 (Jersey 40: PLSC1); JK 8418 (Eastbourne 12: LT9); *JK 8421 (Eastbourne 15: LT9); KW 474 (Blythe and Berwick: PLSC1); KW 1961 (Blythe and Berwick: PLSC3); MN 5107 (Isle of Man 50: LT5A); RP 5979 (United Counties L28: PLSC3); RP 6946 (United Counties L63: PLSC3); RU 8678 (Hants and Dorset 268: PLSC3); TF 818 (Lancashire United 202: LT1); TJ 6760 (Lytham St. Annes 24: LT5A); UP 1533 (Sunderland District 84: PLSC3); VL 1263 (Lincoln 5: LT1); YT 3738 (King George V: PLC1); HF 4535 (Wallasey 8: PLSC1).
*JK 8421 is now registered as LMG 184.

Leyland 'Titan' TD model

In 1927 Leylands introduced one of the first modern double-decker chassis powered by a 6-cylinder 6.8 litre petrol engine. This coincided with the arrival of pneumatic tyres for large vehicles and the relaxation of restriction for top-deck 'canopies' for double-decker motorbuses, and so this new model appealed to many operators, e.g. the municipalities who were thinking of abandoning their tramway systems. The TD1 (plate 12) had a wheelbase of 16 feet 6 inches and could take a body 25 feet long. The wheelbase was reduced to 16 feet 3 inches for the TD5 onwards. A more powerful 7.6 petrol engine was introduced with the TD2 version, and this was replaced by a 6.8 litre oil engine as from the TD5. The more up-to-date parallel-sided radiator was introduced with the TD3 model. The TD6 was specially designed for Birmingham Corporation, but none have survived. The final version, the TD7 with its more flexible engine mountings, arrived at the outbreak of the Second World War. Some 'Titans' had fully automatic transmission, bore the word 'Gearless' on their radiator grilles, and have the suffix 'c' added to the model type.

Preserved examples
ABL 766 (Thames Valley 336: TD4); AFY 971 (Southport 143: TD3); AUF 670 (Southdown 970: TD3); BFE 419 (Lincoln 64: TD7); BRM 596 (Cumberland 132: TD4); BTF 25 (Lytham St. Annes 45: TD4c); DLU 400 (London Transport STD 90: TD4); *DR 4902 (Southern National 2849: TD1); DSG 169 (S.M.T.: TD5); EF 7380 (West Hartlepool 36: TD7); EFJ 241 (Exeter 26: TD5); FEL 215 (Bournemouth 32: TD5); FKO 223 (Maidstone and District 293: TD5); GCD 48 (Southdown 248: TD5); HF 9126 (Wallasey 74: TD7c); J 1199 (Jersey 24: TD1); J 6332 (Jersey 25: TD2); JG 8201 (East Kent: TD4); JK 5605 (East-

bourne 95: TD4); JP 4712 (Wigan: TD7); †JUB 29 (Wallace Arnold: TD1); RN 8622 (Ribble 2057: TD5); UF 4813 (Southdown 813: TD1); UF 7428 (Southdown 928: TD2); WH 1553 (Bolton 53: TD1); ZC 714 (Dublin United R1: TD4); CFM 354 (Crosville M52: TD5); LJ 2941 (Hants and Dorset E354: TD1).
*DR 4902 is in livery of Eastern Counties, but never ran as such.
†JUB 29 is a hybrid made up of chassis of Glasgow 72 and body of West Yorkshire K 451.

Leyland 'Titan' PD model

After the experience learnt in the manufacture of tanks and other military equipment during the Second World War Leylands introduced their post-war series of 'Titan' models in 1946 with a much more powerful 7.4 litre diesel engine. The chassis could carry a 26 foot long body with an overall width of 7 feet 6 inches, although a few 8 foot wide PD1/3s were built. A minor variant, that had Metalastik rubber brushes instead of shackle pins on the road spring attachments, was called the PD1A model. In 1948 the PD2/1 appeared on the scene driven by the new, famous Leyland 0.600 engine of 9.8 litres. This was rated at 125 b.h.p., compared with 100 b.h.p. of the PD1. Because there was such an enormous expansion in the bus industry (especially in the realm of the double-decker) in the period 1946—1951, and because most of the remaining tramways were being replaced by motorbus networks, it paid Leylands to offer the PD2 version of the 'Titan' in a great many alternative forms. With some gaps for non-production marks, the PD2 eventually reached the PD2/57 model! Variations included the choice of pneumocyclic, epicyclic or synchromesh gearboxes, vacuum or air brakes, 7 foot 6 inches or 8 foot wide bodies, exposed or so-called 'St. Helens' concealed radiators (suffixed by the letter 'A'), normal weight chassis or lightweight chassis etc. (For fuller details see *Buses and Trolleybuses Since 1945* by David Kaye, Blandford, 1968.) In 1955 a new model, the PD3 appeared: this was 3 feet longer, at 30 feet, and six variations were offered. With further amendments these eventually reached the PD3A/15 before production ceased in the late 1960s.

Preserved examples

CJY 299 (Plymouth 89: PD1); DBU 23 (Oldham 231: PD1); DDR 414 (Plymouth 114: PD1); EDT 703 (Doncaster 94: PD2/1); EF 9590 (W. Hartlepool 70: PD2/3); EKY 558 (Bradford 558: PD2/3); GLJ 957 (Hants and Dorset 1145: PD1A); GTP 986 (Portsmouth 69: PD2/10); HFJ 144 (Exeter 17: PD2/1); HOV 685 (Birmingham 1685: PD2/1); JCD 81 (Southdown 381: PD2/1); JP 6032 (Wigan 34: PD1); JRR 930 (Barton 509: PD1);

JUO 992 (Southern National 2932: PD1A); KGK 548 (London Transport RTW 48: PD2/3); KGU 263 (London Transport RTL 305: PD2/1); KGU 419 (London Transport RTL 343: PD2/1); KPT 909 (Wearmouth: PD2/1); LEV 917 (City Coaches LD1: PD1); MZ 7789 (N. Ireland RB 927: PD2/1); MKH 82 (East Yorkshire 572: PD2/12); MKH 85 (East Yorkshire 575: PD2/12); MLL 685 (London Transport RTL 1323: PD2/1); LLU 957 (London Transport RTW 467: PD2/3); CHF 565 (Wallasey 106: PD 2/10); JRR 751 (Barton 468: PD1); KEL 131 (Bournemouth 131: PD 2/3).

Leyland 'Tiger' TS series

The Leyland 'Tiger' made its debut in 1927, as the single-decker equivalent of the 'Titan'. It was powered by the same 6-cylinder 6.8 litre petrol engine. It had a wheelbase of 17 feet 6 inches, giving it an overall length of 27 feet 6 inches (TS1 model). None of this mark have survived, but we do have some TS2s which were 1 foot 6 inches shorter than the TS1. By 1930 the TS3 version had also appeared on the scene: its vital statistics were:— 16 feet 6 inches (wheelbase), 26 feet (overall length). This made the TS3 suitable for more tortuous country roads than the TS1 and TS2. In 1932 the TS4 with the more powerful 7.6 litre engine appeared, followed the next year by the TS6 with its parallel sided radiators, in place of the slanting-sided one of earlier models of the 'Tiger'. Vacuum-hydraulic brakes were introduced with the TS7, whilst the redesigned dumb-irons first seen in 1937 heralded in the TS8. The fully flexible engine mountings did not appear in the 'Tiger' until 1941: this model being the TS11. A suffix 'c' denoted a gearless version, whilst the suffix 'T' implied that the vehicle had an extra rear trailing axle, being of overall length of 30 feet. A quite advanced form of the 'Tiger' with an 8.6 litre under-floor oil engine, the FEC model, formed the basis for London Transport's TF class of 1939. The normal control version (i.e. the driver placed *behind* the engine) was called the 'Tigress'.

Preserved examples

ATF 477 (Singleton: TS6T); ARU 179 (Hants and Dorset F482: TS7); BAL 610 (East Midlands B10: TS7); CTF 423 (Lancashire United 114: TS8); DF 8420 (Black and White 37: TS2); DKT 16 (Maidstone and District 558: TS7); DUF 179 (Southdown 1179: TS7); EFJ 666 (Exeter 66: TS8); EK 8867 (Wigan 81: TS4); FJJ 774 (London Transport TF77: FEC); FW 5696 (Lincolnshire 368: TS7); FW 5698 (Lincolnshire 370: TS7); JA 5515 (North Western: TS7); JA 7591 (Stockport Welfare Dept.: TS8); JG 9956 (East Kent: TS8); VR 5996 (Manchester 33: TS2); WG 9754 (Alexanders P684: TS11); ZI 1728 (Dublin United 366: TS3);

CHR 485 (Wilts and Dorset 186: TS8); FEH 832 (Potteries 130: TS8).

Leyland 'Tiger' PS series

In 1946 Leyland resumed their production of the 'Tiger' with the PS1 model. This was powered by the Leyland 7.4 litre oil engine, had a wheelbase of 17 feet 6 inches and a width of 7 feet 6 inches. London Transport used it for their TD class of single-deckers for red central routes. Indeed the PS1 helped to retire many aging and poorly maintained pre-war buses and coaches that had been hard worked during the six years of war. In 1949 synchromesh gearboxes were fitted to new 'Tigers' coming off the assembly lines instead of the previously supplied constant mesh gearboxes. Thus was born the PS2/1. Some PS2/1s were powered by the Leyland 9.8 litre oil engine. The PS2/3 had a drop-frame extension, whilst the PS2/5 'Tiger' was the 8 foot wide model. Production of the 'Tiger' ceased in 1954, by which time it had been superseded by the under-floor 'Royal Tiger' and 'Tiger Cub' models.

Preserved examples

BCB 340 (Blackburn 7: PS1); CFN 104 (East Kent: PS1); GZ 7628 (Ulster T.A. 8560: PS1); HTB 656 (Ramsbottom 17: PS1); JLJ 401 (Bournemouth 86: PS2/1); JLJ 402 (Bournemouth 87: PS2/1); JLJ 403 (Bournemouth 88: PS2/1); JOJ 255 (Birmingham 2255: PS2/1); JRR 930 (Barton 509: PS1); JXC 288 (London Transport TD95: PS1); JXC 314 (London Transport TD121: PS1); JXC 323 (London Transport TD130: PS1); KUP 949 (Iveson, Esk: PS1); LFJ 877 (Greenslades, Exeter: PS2/3).

Leyland 'Cub' and 'Cheetah'

Built at their Kingston-upon-Thames factory, the Leyland 'Cub' appeared in 1932, powered by a six-cylinder 4.4 litre petrol engine. The 'Cub' was basically a normal control vehicle, but some were built with forward control. These have a prefix 'S' for 'Side', referring to the relative positions of the driver and the engine. The 'Cub' came in a variety of wheelbases, suitable for seating between 14 and 26 passengers. The KP2 and later KPZ1 models had a wheelbase of 14 feet and could seat 20, whilst the KP3 and later KPZ2 had a wheelbase of 15 feet 6 inches and were ideal for carrying 24 seats. The SKP3 and later SKPZ2 were the largest of the 'Cubs' with a wheelbase of 15 feet 6 inches and seats for 26 passengers. The models bearing a suffix 'Z' began to appear in 1935 when a new light six 4.7 litre engine was fitted. The 'Cubs' were found as one-man operated buses on lightly trafficked routes (e.g.

London Transport used them along the North Downs) or where there were weak bridges (e.g. Southdown used them over the Hayling Island bridge). Another use they were put to was as inter-station half-decker buses during the night in London. They were just the right size for private hire purposes too. The 'Cub' was replaced in 1939 by the 'Cheetah', that had first appeared four years before. This was a hybrid vehicle made up in the main of assemblies from both the 'Cub' and the 'Lion'. It came in a variety of wheelbases of which the LZ2 was 17 feet 7 inches. The power unit was the Leyland Light Six engine, in both its petrol and diesel forms. London Transport took delivery in 1939 of some rear engined 'Cubs' (their CR class) (plate 16).

Preserved examples
CLE 122 (London Transport C94: SKPZ2); CLX 548 (London Transport C111: SKPZ2); CUF 404 (Southdown 4: KPZ1); FXT 120 (London Transport CR13: KP3); HL 7538 (West Riding 464: KPZ2); JU 963 (Brown Bros.: KP3); NMY 556 (Webster, Wigan: LZ2); RN 7824 (Ribble: LZ2); TV 4847 (Skills 11: SKP3).

Post-war Sunbeam trolleybuses

Between 1947 and 1953 Sunbeams (at this date owned by Guy Motors) built 250 of the new E4 model 4-wheeler (plate 27), some of which still bore Karrier maker's plates. The F4 was 26 feet long and normally carried a double-deck body seating between 54 and 60 passengers, although Mexborough and Swinton Traction purchased some bearing 32-seat central-entrance single-decked bodies. The F4 was often powered by 95 h.p. motors that might come from a variety of manufacturers such as Crompton-Parkinson and British Thompson Houston. In 1945 Mr. Edgley Cox, the General Manager of Walsall Corporation managed to persuade the then Ministry of Transport to relax its regulations and allow 2-axle 30 foot long trolleybuses to operate in this country. Thus was born the longer version known as the F4A, and this enabled up to 70 seated passengers to be carried. From 1948 until 1956 Sunbeams produced a 3-axle trolleybus called the S7 (plate 28), which was 30 feet long and normally 8 feet wide, although Huddersfield bought some with bodies only 7 feet 6 inches wide (this model being known as the S7A). The S7 could carry up to 72 seated passengers in ease and was usually powered by a 95 h.p. motor. Due to its additional axle the S7 was heavier than its replacement, the F4A. Thus whereas Reading Corporation Nos. 170—181 (S7s) weighed 10 tons 2 cwts unladen, their Nos. 182—193 (F4As) only tipped the scales at 8 tons $17\frac{1}{2}$ cwts unladen. A fifth post-war Sunbeam model was the 2-axle MF2B, which had been planned as a single-decker but sold as a double-decker in Britain. Some 27 feet long MF2Bs went to Kingston-upon-Hull Corporation, but Bournemouth Corporation proved to be its chief buyer. Indeed their No. 303 was the very last trolleybus to be built in Britain, when it was completed in 1962. The Bournemouth MF2Bs were 30 feet long and weighed two quarters under nine tons.

Preserved examples

ADX 196 (Ipswich 126: F4); ARC 515 (Derby 215: F4); DRC 224 (Derby 224: F4); ERD 145 (Reading 174: S7); ERD 152 (Reading 181: S7); FJW 616 (Wolverhampton 616: F4); GAJ 12 (Tees-side 2: F4); GAJ 15 (Tees-side 5: F4); LTN 501 (Newcastle-upon-Tyne 501: S7); 297 LJ (Bournemouth 297: MF2B); 299 LJ (Bournemouth 299: MF2B); 301 LJ (Bournemouth 301: MF2B); NDH 959 (Walsall 342: F4); 2206 OI (Belfast 246: F4A); PVH 931 (Huddersfield 631: S7); SCH 237 (Derby 237: F4A); TDH 914 (Walsall 864: F4A); VRD 186 (Reading 186: F4A); VRD 193 (Reading 193: F4A); XDH 72 (Walsall 65: F4A); YLJ 286 (Bournemouth 286: MF2B); KVH 219 (Huddersfield 619: 57);; PV 8270 (Ipswich 105: F4A).

RALLIES

In 1962 the first London to Brighton run was held for veteran and vintage commercial vehicles, and since that year this event has been held annually, normally on the first Sunday in May. Across very different terrain is the Trans-Pennine run between Manchester and Harrogate that was inaugurated in 1969: this takes place usually on the second Sunday in August. 1971 was a year in which other such runs started e.g. the Humberbus run from Hull to Scarborough; the St. Leger Historic Commercial Vehicle and Omnibus Rally between Sheffield and Doncaster; the Robin Hood Vintage Transport run between Nottingham and Mansfield. Time will prove whether these will also become hardy annuals.

The second category of rally is the static display, and in this group comes the Grand Transport Extravaganza at Crich, Derbyshire over the late summer bank holiday weekend (in 1971 it was spread over all three days). The Bus of Yesteryear Rally in late May seems to have a different venue each year (e.g. Stratford-upon-Avon in 1970; the South Bank, London in 1971). Others held in 1971 included the Vintage Transport Day at the Dinting Railway Centre (near Glossop), the Godalming Gathering (in Surrey), the Weymouth Bus Rally and Cavalcade (Dorset), and the Dunbar Veteran, Vintage and Post-vintage Rally (Scotland). The newly opened Sandtoft Transport Centre on the Isle of Axholme, Lincolnshire, held its first such rally in September 1971 (plate 28), this being mainly for trolleybuses, but with some motorbuses.

Thirdly there are the open days at transport collections. One of the most popular is the special Sunday opening at the Museum of British Transport at Clapham in London, held in the Spring, and also that at the West of England Transport Collection at Winkleigh Airfield in north Devon about the same time.

WHY NOT HELP THE PRESERVATION MOVEMENT YOURSELF?

If this book has stimulated your interest in past buses, coaches and trolleybuses, perhaps you would like to join one of the growing number of bands of enthusiasts, who are actively acquiring and restoring such vehicles. The following societies carry out these functions.

The Albion Vehicle Preservation Trust,
3 Hamilton Crescent, Bishopton, Renfrewshire.

The British Trolleybus Society,
7 Westdene Crescent, Caversham, Reading, Berkshire RG4 7HD.

The East Anglia Transport Society,
26 Corve Avenue, South Ockendon, Essex RM15 6BA.

The East Midlands Area Omnibus Enthusiasts Society,
93 Main Street, Swithland, Loughborough, Leicestershire LE12 8TG.

The Historic Commercial Vehicle Club,
32 Acland Crescent, London SE5.

The Lincolnshire Vintage Vehicle Society,
21 West Parade, Lincoln.

The London Trolleybus Preservation Society,
39 Mitchell Road, Palmers Green, London N13.

The Midland Counties Public Service Vehicles Restoration Club,
11 Ashby Lane, Moulton, Northampton.

The National Trolleybus Association,
14 Scandrett Close, Henbury, Bristol, BS10 7SS.

The Vintage Transport Association,
2 Chalcrafts, Alton, Hampshire.

The West Riding Transport Society,
16 Spring Street, Marsden, near Huddersfield, Yorkshire.

The Worthing and Southern Counties Historic Vehicle Group,
8 Farm Avenue, Horsham, Sussex.
The Irish Transport Trust,
13 Gilnakirk Crescent, Belfast 5.
The Transport Museum Society of Ireland,
99 Ardcollum Avenue, Artane, Dublin 5.

In addition there are three important societies, which are concerned with the history of these vehicles and their operation, rather than in actually owning vehicles themselves.

The Omnibus Society,
103A Streatham Hill, London SW2.
The P.S.V. Circle,
52 Old Park Ridings, London N21 2ES.
The Transport Ticket Society,
6 Park Way, Pool-in-Wharfedale, Leeds LS21 1LD.

MUSEUMS

Belfast Transport Museum, Witham Street, Belfast: Belfast trolleybus 112, Belfast wartime Daimler double-decker 214.

Birmingham Museum of Science and Industry, Newhall Street, Birmingham 3: Wolverhampton trolleybus 433.

East Anglia Transport Museum, Chapel Road, Carlton Colville, Lowestoft: various trolleybuses from Ashton-under-Lyne, Brighton, Cardiff, Hastings, Ipswich, London, Newcastle.

Edinburgh Transport Museum, Shrubhill Works, Edinburgh 7: Edinburgh Corporation Daimler CVG6 double-decker 135.

Glasgow Transport Museum, 522 Pollokshaw Road, Glasgow: Glasgow Corporation Albion 'Venturer' double-decker B92, Glasgow BUT single-deck trolleybus TBS 13.

Lincoln Transport Museum, Whisby Road, Lincoln: Leyland 'Lions' KW 474 and TF 818, Bolton Corporation Leyland 'Titan' TD1 53, Bradford Corporation Education Committee Leyland 'Badger', Fentiman's Ford Model 'T' market bus, Lincoln Corporation's unique Ruston and Hornsby engined Guy 'Arab' 23, etc.

Montagu Motor Museum, Beaulieu, Hampshire: 1922 Maxwell charabanc, Portsmouth's first trolleybus.

Museum of British Transport, Triangle Place, Clapham, London SW4: the future of the bus, coach and trolleybus exhibits is at the moment in doubt. Some (including London vehicles) are still on show at the time of writing.

Preston Park, Tees-side: Trolleybus T285 and ex-Middlesbrough Corporation Guy 'Arab IV'.

Sandtoft Transport Centre/Westgate Trolleybus Museum, Belton (both on Isle of Axholme, Lincolnshire): a selection of trolleybuses from Bournemouth, Derby, Huddersfield, Manchester, Reading, South Shields, Walsall and other systems.

Transport Museum of Ireland, Dublin: Dublin United Leyland 'Titan' TD4, GNR Gardner-engined single-decker, Belfast trolleybus 168.

BIBLIOGRAPHY

Buses and Trolleybuses before 1919, David Kaye (Blandford, 1972)

Buses and Trolleybuses, 1919 to 1945, David Kaye (Blandford, 1970)

Buses and Trolleybuses since 1945, David Kaye (Blandford, 1968)

The Early Motor Bus, Charles E. Lee (British Railways, 1964)

A History of London Transport Vol. I: Nineteenth Century, T. C. Barker and M. Robbins (George Allen & Unwin, 1963)

History of the Royal Blue Express Services, R. C. Anderson and G. Frankish (David & Charles, 1970)

The Horse Bus as a Vehicle, Charles E. Lee (British Railways, 1968)

Roads and Vehicles, Anthony Brid (Longmans, 1969)

Steam on Common Roads, William Fletcher (David & Charles, reprint 1972).

The Story of Passenger Transport in Britain, J. Joyce (Ian Allan, 1967)

Transport in Jersey, 1787-1961, Michael Ginns (Transport World, 1961)

Transport Museums, Jack Simmons (George Allen & Unwin, 1970)

Transport Preserved, Bryan Morgan (British Railways, 1968)

Trolleybus Trails, J. Joyce (Ian Allan, 1963)

Veteran and Vintage Public Service Vehicles, David Kaye (Ian Allan, 1962)

INDEX

Printed by Maund & Irvine Ltd., Tring, Herts.